IMAGES OF WAR

TANKS & ARMOUR IN THE BATTLE FOR MOSCOW

RARE PHOTOGRAPHS FROM WARTIME ARCHIVES

Ian Baxter

Pen & Sword
MILITARY

First published in Great Britain in 2026 by
PEN & SWORD MILITARY
an imprint of Pen & Sword Books Ltd
Yorkshire – Philadelphia

Typeset by Concept, Huddersfield, West Yorkshire, HD4 5JL.
Printed and bound in England by CPI Group (UK) Ltd, Croydon, CR0 4YY.

The Publisher's authorised representative in the EU for product safety is Authorised Rep Compliance Ltd, Ground Floor, 71 Lower Baggot Street, Dublin D02 P593, Ireland – www.arccompliance.com

For a complete list of Pen & Sword titles please contact
PEN & SWORD BOOKS LTD
47 Church Street, Barnsley, South Yorkshire, S70 2AS, England
E-mail: enquiries@pen-and-sword.co.uk
Website: www.pen-and-sword.co.uk
or
PEN & SWORD BOOKS
1950 Lawrence Road, Havertown, PA 19083, USA
E-mail: uspen-and-sword@casematepublishers.com
Website: www.penandswordbooks.com

Contents

About the Author

Ian Baxter is a military historian who specialises in German twentieth-century military history. He has written more than seventy books, including *Poland: The Eighteen-Day Victory March*; *Panzers in North Africa*; *The Waffen-SS Ardennes Offensive*; *The Western Campaign*; *The 12th SS Panzer Division Hitlerjugend*; *Waffen-SS on the Western Front*; *Waffen-SS on the Eastern Front*; *The Red Army at Stalingrad*; *Elite German Forces of World War II*; *Armoured Warfare: German Tanks of World War II*; *Blitzkrieg*; *Panzer Divisions at War*; *German Armoured Vehicles of World War Two*; *Last Two Years of the Waffen-SS at War*; *German Soldier Uniforms and Insignia*; *German Guns of the Third Reich*; *From Retreat to Defeat: The Last Years of the German Army at War 1943–45* and, most recently, *The Sixth Army and the Road to Stalingrad*.

He has written over a hundred articles, including 'Last days of Hitler', 'Wolf's Lair', 'The Story of the V1 and V2 Rocket Programme', 'Secret Aircraft of World War Two', 'Rommel at Tobruk', 'Hitler's War with his Generals', 'Secret British Plans to Assassinate Hitler', 'The SS at Arnhem', 'Hitlerjugend', 'Battle of Caen 1944', 'Gebirgsjäger at War', 'Panzer Crews', 'Hitlerjugend Guerrillas', 'Last Battles in the East', 'The Battle of Berlin' and many more.

He has also reviewed numerous military studies for publication, supplied thousands of photographs and important documents to various publishers and film production companies worldwide, and he lectures to schools, colleges and universities throughout the United Kingdom and the Republic of Ireland.

Chapter One

Invasion Unleashed

For the invasion of Russia, code-named Barbarossa, the German Army assembled 3 million men, divided into 105 infantry divisions and 32 panzer divisions. There were 3,332 tanks, over 7,000 artillery pieces, 60,000 motor vehicles and 625,000 horses. This force was distributed into three Army Groups. Army Group North, commanded by General Field Marshal Wilhelm Ritter von Leeb, who had assembled his forces in East Prussia on the Lithuanian frontier. His force provided the main spearhead for the advance on Leningrad. Army Group Centre, commanded by Generalfeldmarschall Fedor von Bock, assembled on the 1939 Polish/Russian Frontier, both north and south of Warsaw. Bock's force consisted of 42nd Infantry-Divisions of the 4th and 9th Army and Panzer Group, II and III, and contained the largest number of German infantry and panzer divisions in all three army groups. The objective of Army Group Centre was to spearhead as rapidly as possible eastwards to the city of Smolensk, which commanded the road to the Russian capital, Moscow. Facing this impressive array of German might along the River Dnieper and Dvina were groups of heavily defended fortifications called the Stalin Line. The defenders were the Russian 13th Army of the West Front, and the 20th Army, 21st Army and the 22nd Army of the Supreme Command (STAVKA) Reserve. In the region, around the strategic city of Vitebsk, the 19th Army was ordered to hold on at all costs, whilst the 16th Army was hastily moved in front of Smolensk. It was the threat in the north from 3rd Panzer Army and 39th Panzer Corps that seriously worried the Red Army. Nevertheless, Stalin had called for a Great Patriotic War against the Nazi invader, and every soldier was determined to do his duty and hold their lines to the grim death. As Army Group Centre continued a general push towards Smolensk in early July 1941, the Russians began a more determined defence. Many bridges were blown up and, for the first time, the Red Army units began laying mines to slow down the Germans. To make matters worse for both the infantry and panzer divisions, heavy rain, typical for July in central Russia, suddenly began turning the roads into streaming rivers of mud, and advancing German units found themselves either slowing down to a painful snail's pace or totally immobile for hours at a time. The German delays gave the Soviets time to organize for an armoured counter blow.

On 6 July, the Russians launched their attack in front of Smolensk with the Soviet 20th Army's 7th and 5th Mechanized Corps attacking advancing German troops and armour with 700 tanks. What followed was the battle of Smolensk with Red Army bitterly contesting every part of ground along the Dnieper River.

To meet the Russian force was Guderian's Panzer Group, advancing eastwards, along three separate axes. The most northerly of these ran from the Dnieper crossings below Orsha, along the line Dubrovno-Lyady-Krasny-Smolensk. This was under the 57th Corps, with the 29th Motorized-Division leading the 17th and 18th Panzer-Divisions. In the centre, the 56th Corps advanced from Mogilev with the 10th Panzer-Division, SS Das-Reich, and Guard Battalion of Gross Deutschland. To the south, up the winding valley of Oster, came the 24th Corps, with the 10th Motorized-Division, the 3rd and 4th Panzer-Division, and the cavalry division, all of which were converging toward Smolensk. For the Red Army, the Battle of Smolensk would take place in several phases, divided into distinct operations to halt the German offensive and the armoured pincers.

Despite relatively strong Russian defensive positions, by the second week of July, the 3rd Panzer Group's 20th Panzer Division established a bridgehead on the east bank of the River Dvina and threatened Vitebsk. To the south, away from the main crossings, Panzer Group.II launched surprise attacks forcing the River Dnieper. The Soviet 13th Army was pushed back, losing five divisions. As both German panzer armies drove east, three Soviet Armies – 20th, 19th and 16th, faced the prospect of encirclement around Smolensk.

What followed was intensive fighting. Armour and troops from the 29th Motorized Infantry Division blasted their way through towards the city in a series of successive attacks. Soviet soldiers either fought to the death or saved themselves by escaping the impending slaughter by withdrawing to another makeshift position. In the early morning of 16 July, fighting intensified with even greater losses to the Russians. The battles that took place in and around Smolensk became a fierce contest of attrition, and although the Russians showed great fortitude and determination, they were constantly hampered by lack of weapons and manpower needed to sustain them on the battlefield. Consequently, the remaining troops holding out in the city were subjected to merciless ground and aerial bombardments. The situation for the defenders looked grim. The ferocity of the German attack was immense and without respite. After nearly twenty-four hours of almost continuous battle, the Russian soldiers had become exhausted. Stalin's insistence that his troops must fight from fixed positions without any tactical retreat had consequently caused many units to become encircled, leaving tank units to speed past unhindered and achieve even deeper penetrations.

By the early afternoon of 16 July, Smolensk was finally captured by 29th Motorized-Infantry-Division. In the north, Hoth's Panzer Group III was moving much more slowly. The terrain was swampy and the rain was still hampering operations in a number of places. The Russians were fighting desperately to escape the trap that was developing. On 18 July, the great armoured pincers of the two German panzer armies came within 10 miles of closing the gap. But the jaws would not finally snap shut and bitter fighting raged for more than a week.

Whilst the battle of Smolensk raged and the Germans tried liquidating the Smolensk pocket with some 500,000 Soviet troops fighting inside, General Guderian immediately set about implementing plans to crush Soviet forces, further east around the town of Roslavl. The operation had taken the Red Army by complete surprise. The sudden speed and depth of the German attack was a brilliant display of all-arms coordination. The Soviets were quite unprepared for the might of the German attack. In some areas along the front, units were simply brushed aside and totally destroyed. Red Army survivors recalled that they had been caught off guard, lulled into a false sense of security after escaping from the Smolensk pocket. Now they were being attacked by highly mobile armour and blasted by heavy artillery. In many places, the force of attack was so heavy that they were unable to organize any type of defence. In total confusion, hundreds of troops, disheartened and frightened, retreated to avoid the slaughter, whilst other more fanatical units remained ruthlessly defending their positions to the death. On 1 August, Guderian's force launched his Roslavl offensive. The Russian force that was thrown in to the German attack comprised remnants from the battle of Smolensk. They were completely exhausted, short of ammunition and vulnerable.

The Russians tried desperately to hold onto the town of Roslavl, but under direct attack by seven fresh German infantry divisions, the defence soon crumbled away. Around the town, a pocket soon began to form, with Germans bringing up greater artillery concentration, whilst Red Army troops feebly tried to break out. Roslavl finally fell to the Germans on 3 August. Guderian ordered a panzer striking force of three divisions immediately. They were ordered away from the main battle to probe southwards and clear up stragglers from both Smolensk and Roslavl.

The battles of Smolensk and Roslavl were one of the swiftest and most complete German Army victories in the East. Altogether some 300,000 Soviet soldiers had been captured in the Smolensk pocket. However, 200,000 had managed to break out and fight in Roslavl and surrounding areas further east.

By the end of the summer, Hitler was confident that he would soon secure victory in the centre. For this reason, he ordered that Army Group Centre be assigned to operations against Moscow. The forces committed to the operation were immense. They included the 2nd, 4th and 9th Infantry armies supported by three well equipped Panzer Groups which comprised of the 2nd, 3rd, and 4th. In the air, Luftflotte 2 were to be used to strike enemy positions in order to wrench open the front and allow the armoured spearhead to pour through. Some 2 million German soldiers were committed to the attack along with 1,000–2,470 tanks and assault guns and 14,000 guns. The tactical plan for the attack once again relied on 'blitzkrieg' strategy, using its powerful armoured forces to drive deep into the Red Army lines and execute double-pincer movements, where they would surround whole Red Army divisions and annihilate them.

Facing this massive assemblage of German infantry and armoured formations were three Soviet fronts that were heavily defending positions between the cities of Vyazma and Bryansk. It was this defensive line that blocked the road to Moscow. In spite of the vast array of German armour on the central front, the Russians still had a formidable concentration of men, armour and guns. Some 1,250,000 men, 1,000 tanks and 7,600 guns were dug-in along the front.

General Moritz Albrecht Franz Friedrich Fedor von Bock commander of Army Group Centre for the invasion of Russia. He is seen here on the left during the summer of 1941. Bock was relieved of his command by Hitler after the failure to take Moscow, known as 'Operation Typhoon' and then the German retreat from the Red Army in July 1942. He was then compelled into retirement for the rest of the war. *(Bundesarchiv Bild 101I-265-0048A-03)*

Two photographs showing both Wehrmacht and Luftwaffe prime movers loaded onto special flat bed rail cars destined for the Eastern Front prior to the invasion of the Soviet Union.

Wehrmacht troops pose on top of a Pz.Kpfw.III. For the invasion of Russia, the Germans had a total of 965 Pz.Kpfw.IIIs. During the first half of the war, the Pz.Kpfw.III was certainly a match for its opponent's tanks and quickly and effectively demonstrated its superiority on the battlefield. In fact, it played a crucial part in the advance on Moscow.

A Luftwaffe flak crew wearing standard issue army greatcoats stand in front of their prime mover during operations through central Russia.

A crewman of a Pz.Kpfw.I can be seen in a forest area. Russia was the final campaign for this light tank, which formed a large portion of armoured strength. Whilst the armoured drive through central Russia in the summer of 1941 was successful, Pz.Kpfw.I crews soon found out how inferior these tanks were against the newer Russian models, such as the medium T-34 and heavy KV tanks.

A column of prime movers towing ordnance along a congested road bound for the front in July 1941.

A spectacular sight showing a panzer division spread out across a field during operations in the summer of 1941. There are a variety of armoured and support vehicles that can be seen including Pz.Kpfw.IIs, III & IV including StuG.III and Pz.Kpfw.35(t) and 38(t).

A prime mover hauling a 10.5cm leFH 18 infantry gun towards the front. This leichte Feldhaubitze or light field howitzer was the standard artillery piece of the Wehrmacht.

A StuG.III advances along a typical Russian road. By this early period of the war, armoured crews had learnt that the Sturmgeschütz demonstrated limitations when fighting took place, especially during close quarter contact.

With the lack of roads in central Russia, armoured vehicles often struggled and as a result often slowed down various units. In this photograph, a prime mover is towing a wheeled vehicle along a sandy road.

Officers smile for camera from their Kubelwagen car. These cars were probably one of the most famous German vehicles during the war. They had a strong chassis; they were simple and reliable, rugged with good cross-country performances.

A column of Pz.Kpfw.III was an ultimate credit to the panzer divisions it served. The crews that rode and fought in this vehicle from the Blitzkrieg days of Poland and France, to its successful drive through central Russia in the summer of 1941, were proud of its effectiveness and reliability on the battlefield.

Two shirtless crew members stand in front of their prime mover during a lull in their advance. These Sonderkraftfahrzeug or special motorized vehicles were mainly used to haul heavy ordnance such as the 21cm Morser, 15cm howitzer or the 10.5cm or 8.8cm flak gun.

A StuG.III crosses a pontoon bridge. In the Soviet Union, the StuG operated in close support of the infantry, following behind the advancing troops and providing high explosive artillery fire to help overcome any enemy strong points that were holding up the advance.

A column of Pz.Kpfw.IIs roll along a road. Although this panzer had originally been designed as a stopgap solution while larger, more advanced tanks were developed, it nonetheless played an important role on the Eastern Front in 1941.

A prime mover towing a 15cm schwere Feldhaubitze 18 or sFH 18 field howitzer across a wooden pontoon.

A StuG.III complete with scissor binoculars can be seen along a dusty road with two soldiers that have hitched a lift, one of which appears to be injured. The vehicles main task was to suppress heavy infantry and anti-tank weapons that could not be destroyed by heavy infantry weapons.

A StuG Ausf.B laden with supplies has halted near a river crossing. During the summer of 1941, the StuG acquitted itself very well in its first actions in Russia. However, the lack of a machine gun for close support against enemy infantry was a problem with early variants.

A StuG.III hurtles along a dusty round during the summer of 1941. For the invasion of Russia, German factories had completed 548 StuG.III vehicles. The StuG had a crew of four and came equipped with a 7.5cm StuK 37 L/24 gun capable of traversing from 12.5 degrees left to 12.5 degrees right.

Vehicles and cyclists cross a heavy pontoon bridge known by the Germans as a Bruckengerat B. The pontoon boats have been lashed together and the bridging deck sections secured over them in order to allow traffic and soldiers on foot to pass over.

Wehrmacht troops survey destroyed Soviet tanks during their advance. Despite the success of the initial German spearheads through central Russia, as columns edged deeper into the Soviet heartlands, resistance increased, putting more strain on some of the more overstretched units.

Infantry support vehicles advance along a road passing a dead horse. It was estimated that some 300,000 horses were used for the advance through central Russia towards Moscow, with many of the animals being utilized to tow equipment and ordnance to the front. The Landser relied heavily on draught animals for motive power. Although the infantry regiments were supplied with light trucks to move ordnance and other equipment to the front, many infantry regiments, especially those recently raised divisions, relied heavily on horses. Motorized prime movers were preferred, as it was necessary to rapidly move weapons and supplies from position to position in order to survive and effectively engage the enemy.

Chapter Two

Operation Typhoon

Over the days and weeks that followed, the Soviet Army were overwhelmed by the German onslaught. It now seemed that Hitler's grand strategy had yielded such astonishing results that the Eastern Front would soon be conquered. Emboldened by these victorious gains in mid-September, Hitler once again began drawing up his plans for the resumption of operations against Moscow. On 16 September, the panzers were finally halted, and their withdrawal to the Moscow front began in earnest.

The regrouping for the final assault on Moscow was a massive logistical nightmare, as three Panzer Groups, Guderian, Hoth and Hoppner, were to be used. Of these, Hoth's panzer force was already in place, while Guderian's had to make the long haul back from the Ukraine, and the Hoppner tanks transferred from the Leningrad front. Within two weeks, Bock's forces were in place and ready for action

During the early hours of 30 September 1941, the first phase of the attack on Moscow began, code-named 'Operation Typhoon'. The assault began with Panzer Group II being launched north-eastwards towards Orel, from where it would thrust north behind Yeremenko's Bryansk Front. Two days later, on 2 October, the rest of the Army Group rolled forward with more than 2,000 tanks bearing down on the Soviet capital. Along Bock's entire central front, panzer and infantry poured a storm of fire into the dwindling Red Army ranks. Within hours of the initial attack, the Russian front was already in landslide. However, the deeper Bock's forces advanced, the heavier the resistance grew. In front of Moscow, the Russians had constructed formidable defences in preparation for the German assault on their capital. Thousands of tanks and artillery were placed in the ground up to their gun barrels. Many thousands of mines were laid in the path of the German armoured spearhead. Nearly a million anti-personnel mines and booby traps were set up to explode and kill or maim unsuspecting German infantry. In towns and cities along the road leading to Moscow, the Russians erected thousands of crude defence barriers.

Although Bock's advance went well, the mass of infantry, consisting of the 2nd, 4th, and 9th Armies, found it difficult to maintain pace with the fast-moving armour. Consequently, the bulk of them encountered fierce resistance with intense savage fighting in many areas. To make matters worse, on 6 October, the weather began to change as cold driving rain fell on Army Group Centre. Within hours, the Russian countryside had been turned into a quagmire with roads and fields becoming virtually impassable. All the roads leading to Moscow had become boggy swamps. Although tracked vehicles managed to push forward through the mire at a slow pace, trucks and other wheeled vehicles were hopelessly stuck up to their axles in deep, boggy mud. Within a month, the operation had gone from a rapid drive to a slow crawl. During this period, Army Group Centre had lost nearly 35,000 men, excluding the sick and injured, about 240 tanks and heavy artillery pieces, and over 800 vehicles. Surprisingly, the majority of the tanks and other vehicles had not fallen foul to enemy fire, but were lost to the muddy terrain. Supplies were now becoming dangerously low, and fuel and ammunition were hardly adequate to meet the ever-growing demands of the drive to Moscow. With no prospect of reaching the capital before November, concerns began to grow among many of the commanders about the lack of winter supplies.

Despite the mire that reduced virtually the entire central front to a crawl, the weather improved slightly, which allowed the spearheads of the 3rd and 4th Panzer Groups to overrun enemy defences at Vyazma on 10 October. What followed was a series of wide sweeping pincer movements which trapped the Red Armies 16th, 19th, 20th, 24th and elements of the 32nd. Even though they were encircled, the Russians continued to fight with determined ferocity. The fighting was so vicious it drew in some twenty-eight German divisions to try to destroy them, many of these were being used to support the offensive towards Moscow. What remained of the Russian formations defending their positions retreated, breaking through the pocket in a number of places near the town of Mozhaisk. Although there were considerable losses, some of the units escaped intact and joined forces defending Moscow. Some were even strong enough to counterattack which included an ambush near the town of Mtsensk against a battle group belonging to the 4th Panzer Division by the hastily formed 1st Guards Special Rifle Corps supported by the 4th Tank Brigade. The heaviest tanks in the 4th Panzer arsenal comprised of Pz.Kpfw.IVs, and these were attacked by newly built T-34 tanks that had cleverly hidden in the surrounding forests. What shocked the panzer crews was that the Russian T-34's were almost impervious to German tank guns. During the ambush nine panzers were lost, with six completely destroyed, and three damaged.

Other Red Army forces counterattacked in the area which further hindered the advanced echelons of the armoured spearheads from achieving their daily objectives. The German 2nd Army, which was operating to north of Guderian's units with the sole aim of encircling the Bryansk Front, also came under a heavy barrage of enemy resistance.

Despite the heavy fighting and strong enemy opposition, the Germans had successfully captured over 500,000 soldiers in both the Vyazma and Bryansk pockets. The operations were hailed as a completed success and Hitler now put into place, optimistically, the imminent destruction of enemy forces defending in front of Moscow. However, unbeknown to the Führer the Red Army were making massive efforts to increase defence outside the Russian capital. Georgy Zhukov, recalled from the Leningrad Front, was put in charge of Moscow's defence which included using the Western and Reserve Fronts. Stalin then ordered the evacuation of the Communist Party, the General Staff and various civil government offices from Moscow to Kuibyshev, leaving only a number of officials inside the city. Outside the city the Mozhaisk defence line of fortifications had been built on the western approaches to Moscow, and was manned by 90,000 soldiers, Zhukov decided to use the line not as a main defensive position but to concentrate at four critical points where his forces could defend various strategic towns. At the same time, he ordered 250,000 women and teenagers to build a string of trenches and anti-tank moats around Moscow. In a matter of weeks, the civilians moved almost 3 million cubic metres of earth using mainly shovels.

By 12–13 October, the Germans resumed their offensive against Moscow. The 3rd Panzer Army immediately became embroiled in heavy fighting but reported it had captured the town of Volokolmask. Following heavy fighting, advanced elements cut the Kalinin Klin highway only 40 miles north of Moscow. In the south, tanks from the 4th Panzer Army managed to strike forward against desperate Russian resistance and smash its way through to Naro Fominsk. However, some hours later, they were halted by blown bridges across the Moscow River. On the southern sector of the front, despite high losses in men and materiel, Guderian's force bypassed the doomed city of Tula and succeeded driving north-east, capturing the small towns of Venev and Stalinogorsk.

By 29 October, advanced elements of Bock's central front were now within grasp of Moscow. With German units approaching the city limits, the Red Army's 1st Guards Cavalry Corps was ordered to undertake a counteroffensive along with the 10th Army, 49th Army and 50th Army, who were protecting the flanks and attacking from Tula. On 31 October, the German High Command ordered a halt to all offensive operations against Moscow until numerous logistical problems were resolved and enemy defences were neutralised.

(**Above**) Motorcycle combinations belonging to a Kradschützen Battalion in September 1941. In a panzer division, a typical KradSchützen Battalion comprised of a Battalion Headquarters of three motorcycle rifle companies, one motorcycle MG company, and one heavy company. Each motorcycle rifle company consisted of eighteen light machine guns, two heavy machine guns, and three 5cm mortars. It also had a machine gun company of eight heavy machine guns and six 8cm mortars. During the first months of the war on the Eastern Front, the Kradschützen truppen enjoyed much success bucketing across dry open fields and along the hard sun-baked roads. The motorcycles were versatile, fast, and able to go places more readily than other means of transport such as trucks, armoured fighting vehicles, horses, and wagons. The Kradschützen truppen were used in Russia as courier dispatches, scouting operations, transporting and escorting officers, carrying riflemen, and hunting and destroying enemy armoured vehicles. Even as the weather changed and driving rain turned roads into a quagmire, the bikes could cope better with the antiquated boggy roads than any other vehicle. However, when the snow and freezing winter arrived, even the Kradschützen Battalions became stagnated along the front lines. Although there had been considerable success during the summer months, motorcycle troops had suffered heavy casualties during the campaign, as they did not have the protection or firepower to exist as a separate battalion.

(**Opposite, above**) A Pz.Kpfw.IV moves across an open field creating dust. The Pz.Kpfw.IV became the most popular panzer in the Panzerwaffe and remained in production throughout the war. Originally, the Pz.Kpfw.IV was designed as an infantry support tank, but soon proved to be so diverse and effective that it earned a unique offensive and defensive role on the battlefield.

(**Opposite, below**) A Pz.Kpfw.III advances along a road. In the summer of 1941, the Pz.Kpfw.III was by far the largest contingent of armour to fight in Russia. Although the Pz.Kpfw.III was very successful, the vast distances which these tanks had to cover eventually limited its tactics, as well as causing breakdowns and immense supply problems.

A prime mover hauling an 8.8cm FlaK gun crosses a heavy pontoon bridge known by the Germans as a Bruckengerat B.

A column of Pz.Kpfw.IIs advance along a road. During the summer of 1941, the Pz.Kpfw.II demonstrated that this light tank was so seriously under-gunned and under-armoured that it could not fight effectively on the Eastern Front.

Two photographs showing a reconnaissance mission with an Sd.Kfz.221/222 light armoured car. The first image shows the Sd.Kfz.222 halted on a road with supporting infantry, whilst the other photograph, an Sd.Kfz.221 complete with MG 34, shows the vehicle on the move. As the war progressed on the Eastern Front, reconnaissance battalions become highly mobile motorized infantry with panzer divisions supported by the Volkswagen Kubelwagens and Sd.Kfz.221/222/223 light armoured cars. As with all German combat formations, the composition of the Aufklärungsabteilung varied from division to division. Generally though, in the first year of the war in Russia, a typical Aufklärungsabteilungen attached to a panzer division, was equipped with armoured vehicles, with all troops transported in half-tracks.

A Pz.Kpfw.III can be seen moving along a muddy track with 20-litre 'Jerry' cans festooned to the top of the turret. The long distances in which these vehicles travelled constantly required the crews to halt for fuel.

An Sd.Kfz.223 radio vehicle crosses a bridge. Initially its frame antenna comprised of a 30-watt FuG 10 medium-range radio set; and later versions of the vehicle were equipped with an improved 80-watt FuG 12 radio set.

A column of Pz.Kpfw.IIIs advance along a road bound for the front.

A prime mover has just crossed a heavy pontoon Bruckengerat B bridge.

Vehicles have halted on a typical Russian road in the Oral sector of the front during the drive on Moscow in October 1941. In western Russia the all-weather roads had not been constructed to carry the amount and weight of traffic that now used them and the surfaces began to break up under the strain, creating muddy roads.

A motorized column advances along a road bound for the Soviet capital.

German infantry pose for the camera with a halted Pz.Kpfw.IV. It was quite common practice for troops to hitch a lift on a tank and be transported into battle where they would dismount and go into action.

Winter-clad infantry can be seen standing next to their prime mover wearing standard German infantry-issue greatcoats.

An Sd.Kfz.223 radio vehicle along with other vehicles struggles through the mire following a downpour of rain. These armoured cars were intended for reconnaissance and screening. They scouted ahead of mechanized units to assess enemy strength and location. Their primary role was to observe rather than fight enemy units, although they were expected to fight enemy reconnaissance elements when required.

A prime mover can be seen towing a support vehicle along a muddy road. These struggling vehicles belong to the 20th Panzer Division.

A prime mover is towing a stricken Sd.Kfz.221 through the mud. These vehicles belong to the 4th Panzer-Division. On 3 October 1941, the Division arrived at Orel, following successful attacks from the town of Kromy. This had been a battle of attrition, with serious losses in men and equipment.

A halftrack tows a bus used for supplying troops and materials to the front along a muddy road. German forces utilized various types of buses for a range of military purposes. These included transporting soldiers, serving as ambulances, acting as command and control centres, and even as mobile post offices. Some buses were specifically manufactured for the military, while others were repurposed civilian vehicles.

An Sd.Kfz.10 belonging to the 20th Panzer-Division advances along an icy road. For the panzer divisions in Army Group Centre, mud was a formidable foe. The mud produced from a few hours of rain was enough to turn a relatively typical uneven Russian road into a quagmire.

A Horch vehicle during a tyre change has had straw applied to the bonnet in order to protect the engine from freezing. The Horch brand of vehicles, particularly the Horch 901 and Horch 108, were used extensively on the Eastern Front. These off-road vehicles were used for various purposes, including personnel transport, staff car duties, and towing light to medium guns. The Horch 901, for instance, was a versatile 4 × 4 personnel carrier, while the Horch 108 was a rugged vehicle capable of towing light artillery pieces.

Winter-clad German infantry stand in the snow. The photographer has taken a photograph of the soldiers standing next to a Sd.Kfz.263. This German armoured vehicle was specifically a heavy armoured radio car (Panzerfunkwagen). It was based on the chassis of the Sd.Kfz.231 (8-Rad) and Sd.Kfz.232 (8-Rad) armoured cars.

Two crew members of a Pz.Kpfw.IV stand next to their vehicle. At first, virtually all of the German vehicles fighting on the Eastern Front did not receive any type of winter whitewash paint and retained their original dark grey camouflage scheme, making them more susceptible to attack in the snow.

Two photographs taken in sequence showing Pz.Kpfw.IVs operating on the Eastern Front during the winter of 1941. This tank was a versatile and reliable vehicle that served as the backbone of the German panzer divisions on all fronts.

A motorized column advances along a road bound for the Soviet capital. The photograph has been taken from the rear of a vehicle which is towing a 2cm FlaK gun.

A Pz.Kpfw.III advances through the snow supporting infantry towards the front. An MG 34 machine gunner can be seen.

An interesting photograph showing a column of Sd.Kfz.10/5 halftracks halted along a snowy road. The Sd.Kfz.10/5 was a self-propelled anti-aircraft gun based on the Sd.Kfz.10 half-track chassis. It mounted a 2cm FlaK 38 anti-aircraft gun, and saw service with both the Luftwaffe and Wehrmacht units through the war.

A concealed Sd.Kfz.10/5 mounting a 2cm FlaK gun can be seen in the snow partially covered by white sheeting in order to help mask it in the snow.

A motorcycle combination leads a column of supply trucks along a road that has evidently been blown by Russian engineers in their attempt to hinder movement of enemy traffic. As German forces advanced nearer to the Soviet capital, the Russians became more determined than ever to stem the German onslaught by any means possible, from blowing bridges, laying endless anti-tank traps, mining and destroying main roads.

(**Above**) Motorcycle combinations and support vehicles advance along a road crossing a wooden bridge over a frozen river. By November 1941, approximately 800 vehicles had been lost in Army Group Centre, most of which had not fallen foul to enemy fire, but due to the severe weather.

(**Opposite, above**) Outside the town of Ruza and a column of Pz.Kpfw.IIIs can be seen halted along with supporting Pz.Kpfw.IIs.

(**Opposite, below**) Infantrymen survey a knocked out Soviet KV-II heavy tank. This massive tank was armed with a 152mm M-1938/40 L/20 howitzer in a high, box turret with all-round traverse, upon the KV-I hull. Despite the impressive fire-power, the vehicle was notoriously unreliable in the summer defensive campaigns of 1941. As a result, the majority of KV-II were removed from combat duties after the first summer operations against the Germans.

Troops clutching their mess tins can be seen queuing at the rear of a supply truck in the snow. By October 1941, the Germans strove desperately to develop and dispatch items of clothing that would not only help camouflage their troops in the snow, but would help protect them against the cold climate as well.

German infantry and a motorcyclist survey what appears to be a decimated Sd.Kfz.221 armoured reconnaissance vehicle.

A typical scene on the road to Moscow in late 1941, showing vehicles stuck in the snow. All across the front hundreds of tanks and armoured vehicles had become mired, and as result, the majority were simply abandoned in the drifting snow. By mid-December, with the situation worse than ever, the temperatures reached 40 degrees below zero. Despair gripped Army Group Centre.

An Sd.Kfz.10/4 mounting a 2cm FlaK 30 had been involved in some action. The sides of the halftrack are folded down, thus allowing extra space on board the halftrack for the flak crew.

Chapter Three

Road to Disaster

Though the advancing armoured spearheads of Army Group Centre had achieved successful penetrations against the enemy on the road to Moscow, their rapid speed had outstripped supplies causing advancing units to halt. Another problem was that much of the motive power in the German arsenal was still dependent on draught animals, comprising of hundreds of thousands of horses, which consequently slowed the advance. When the rain showers came in early autumn and the bad road system was turned to mud, no one in the German command had anticipated the problems of how to deal with the situation. Instead, horses, wheeled vehicles, and soldiers with their equipment ground to a halt in the quagmire. For hours, and sometimes days, units fought to try to rescue their men and equipment. Tracked vehicles were often withdrawn from the line and brought back to tow stricken soldiers, sometimes up to their waist in mud trying to relieve vehicles and horses.

By late October, conditions in Army Group Centre had deteriorated considerably. During the last two weeks of the month, weather conditions became much worse. Heavy rain, snow showers, and enveloping mists made movement almost impossible for Bock's forces. In front of these exhausted troops stood General Zhukov's men, who were determined to defend Moscow to the last. Even when the Germans managed to breakthrough their lines, the Russian rear guards never left their position until they were literally blown off it. Slowly, the movement of the panzers halted through fatigue, shortages, and the freezing climate. The Soviets then exploited the situation and attacked them without respite, pulverising their positions with their Katyusha rocket mortars.

The conditions were hardly compatible with what the German infantryman panzer crews had trained for. When the first snow showers came in October 1941, no one in the Panzerwaffe could comprehend how much worse the situation would become. Units had been in action, without relief, since June, and the thinness of the front line meant that it was too fragile for whole divisions to withdraw to rest and refit. Instead, units would sit along the front and endure a winter unparalleled to anything ever experienced thus far.

During this period, Army Group Centre had lost nearly 35,000 men, excluding the sick and injured, about 240 tanks and heavy artillery pieces, and over 800 vehicles. Surprisingly, the majority of the tanks and other vehicles had not fallen foul to enemy fire, but were lost to the muddy terrain. As a consequence, supplies were now becoming dangerously low, and fuel and ammunition were hardly adequate to meet the ever-growing demands of the drive to Moscow. With still no prospect of reaching the capital before November, concerns began to grow among many of the commanders about the lack of winter supplies.

By early November, German supply lines were so overstretched, their vehicles were breaking down, and casualty returns were mounting by the hour. Stagnating in front of Moscow, Bock stated that he would have to regroup Army Group Centre for the final march on the capital. Yet, several days later on 15 and 16 November, his army group, still exhausted and under strength, was ordered by Hitler to push forward toward Moscow and capture the city before the snow blizzards arrived in December. At first, the advance went well and Hoth's Panzer Group threatened to break open the whole Russian position in the northwest. To the south Guderian's force also came close to achieving its objective. But the freezing temperatures had caused well over half of frost bite casualties in each of the regiments of the 4th Panzer Division. Slowly, the division deteriorated in the snow, and by the end of November was near to collapse. With the almost total destruction of Guderian's force he ordered his men to a fight a defensive battle of attrition in the terrible arctic conditions.

In spite of the terrible state of Army Group Centre, Hitler ordered that Bock should continue with their drive on Moscow regardless of the terrible shortages in men and materiel. Day by day, the ingredients of disaster grew. By early December, the situation became much worse as the temperature dropped. Many soldiers were now reluctant to emerge from their shelter during the blizzards to fight. Hundreds of tanks were abandoned in the drifting snow. By mid-December, the situation deteriorated further as the temperatures reached 40 degrees below zero. Despair gripped Army Group Centre. On Christmas Eve, Guderian had less than forty panzers in his entire command; Hoppner had no more than fifteen tanks, and they were still told not to withdraw.

Across the entire German front in Army Group Centre, virtually all units had frozen into immobility. The army that had swept into the Russian heartlands only six months earlier were now surrounded by icy wastes and were either reduced to a painful and struggling crawl or had halted abruptly in the snow. If a unit did have the manpower resources and equipment to undertake an assault, their attacks were not like the Russian Army who massed thousands of infantry. It was often undertaken by small groups of soldiers and supporting armour, making desperate efforts to achieve almost impossible objectives. They were regularly fighting against an enemy that were well-suited for winter warfare. Weakened by privation and exertion, German units were overrun along parts of the crumbling front. In certain parts of the front, some units had to undertake a desperate retreat which was often fought by soldiers frightened by the hostility in severe weather conditions. There was also a fear of being wounded and left behind in the subzero temperatures, which often meant death.

Despite the dire situation in which Bock's forces were placed, Hitler's policy, to hold his battered frost-bitten forces in front of Moscow, had in fact saved ground, but at an alarming expenditure in men and materiel. The Russians, as predicted, finally ran out of power because of the harsh weather, and were unable to achieve any deep penetration into the German lines. This had consequently saved Army Group Centre from complete destruction. Although Hitler would later say that the battle for Moscow was his finest hour, his army had in fact failed to capture the city, being crucified by Russian winter and by fanatical Soviet resistance. But much of the failure of Operation Typhoon was essentially due to the remarkable Russian recovery and their winter offensive. The battle had completely altered the German war machine from its glorious days in June and July 1941. From now on, it was to carry the scars of the battle of Moscow to its grave.

A typical scene on the road to Moscow showing wheeled vehicles struggling to advance. The terrible road system plagued seemingly endless miles of terrain.

This road has been reduced to a mud track and soldiers struggle to move a stranded vehicle. Note the letter 'E' painted in yellow on the vehicle's left fender indicating the divisional symbol of the 20th Panzer-Division.

An 8.8cm Luftwaffe flak crew can be seen in the snow in late 1941 with what appears to be a brand new piece of ordnance being towed by a prime mover. The 8.8cm FlaK gun saw continuous use on the Eastern Front in late 1941, and was such an effective weapon that it would be extensively used throughout the rest of the war, scoring sizeable hits against both ground and air targets.

A typical scene in front of Moscow included drifting snow and German vehicles unable to advance any further. In this photograph, German infantry stand next to a half-submerged Horch vehicle during a blizzard. The German High Command had not anticipated a long, drawn-out battle for Moscow and predicted in its planning that the war would be won by October at the very latest. Now troops were compelled to fight in the winter with drastic measures taken to help protect them against the arctic conditions.

German pioneers can be seen in a prime mover hauling a trailer which carries a motorcycle and parts of a bridging section.

In the snow, an Sd.Kfz.7 can be seen with a 21cm Mrs 18 Morser on tow. These weapons were purposely designed to fire projectiles at higher than normal angles of elevation for long-range firing. They could inflict considerable damage on enemy lines and were used extensively on the Ostfront to destroy fortifications, bunkers systems, and any other enemy defensive position.

An Sd.Kfz.7 with mounted flak gun can be seen advancing along a road passing winter-clad infantry wearing early style winter snow overalls and jackets. By November 1941, large batches of winter garments, comprised of different styles of white, lightweight covers, were hastily dispatched to the front-line combat troops. There were snow shirts, two-piece snow suits, snow overalls, and the single-piece snow overall. As the bitter temperatures dropped during late November and early December, further attempts by the troops to improvise on their winter wear increased, including the use of animal skin coats and captured Russian stocks of clothes, which were often lined with fur.

Two photographs taken in sequence showing a Pz.Kpfw.III halted in the snow. The tank is armed with the upgraded 5cm KwK 38 L/42 main gun. The upgraded gun was directly in response to increasingly better armed and armoured opponents. The later Pz.Kpfw.III Ausf.F to Ausf.J were upgraded with the 5cm KwK 38 L/42.

A well-stocked Pz.Kpfw.III can be seen in the snow using a building for concealment against enemy observation. Note all the supplies and provisions secured on the vehicle's engine deck.

A column of Pz.Kpfw.III Ausf.J belonging to the 12th Panzer Division. These variants which were introduced in March 1941 were armed with a 5cm KwK 38 L/42 tank gun. It used the same Maybach HL 120 TRM petrol/gasoline 285 horsepower engine and had identical armour thickness as the Ausf.G. The frontal hull's basic armour thickness had increased to 5cm. An additional armour plate was installed internally to the front of the turret in the spring of 1941, increasing it to a maximum thickness of 5.7cm in places.

A StuG.III Ausf.E has become stuck in a frozen river. This Ausf.E was the final production variant of this iconic SPG featuring the short barrelled 7.5cm gun for use in infantry support roles.

What appears to be a knocked out Red Army KV-1 heavy tank. In 1941 this tank was far superior to any German tank in service. By the time of the German invasion of Russia there were twenty-nine mechanized Soviet corps but these were largely destroyed in the opening battles.

Two photographs showing troops trying to release their vehicles from the quagmire. Due to the appalling road conditions, the use of the main roads was restricted generally to priority class vehicles such as tanks and halftracks. Next in priority came the ammunition columns and fuel convoys, and then the reinforcements needed to nourish the advance. The nearer to the battle zones, the worse the road system often became.

A heavy Horch cross-country vehicle advances slowly along a muddy road towing a 3.7cm PaK 35/36. German commanders observed with alarm how roads vanished in just a few hours of rain and soon realized how dependent they were on the few all-weather roads built in western Russia.

A German Caterpillar Tractor can be seen towing a support truck along a muddy road. The Soviet Union proved to be a completely alien environment to the German war machine, and the distances travelled soon proved more problematic than ever imagined. Russia would not only test the endurance of the German soldier's physical stamina, but also his weapons and supplies. The Panzer-waffe too were pushed almost to the end of their endurance on the road to Moscow with the mud, snow, and then the spring thaw, which again turned all the roads into a quagmire.

Even as the roads began to dry out following the spring thaw, movement was often hazardous and slow for both draught animals and vehicles. These three photographs show the condition of the road system with improved weather.

Along a muddy road horses are seen towing a HF 12 small kitchen wagon. These small mobile kitchens could operate on the move, cooking stews, soups, and coffee. The limber carried utensils and equipment. The troops nicknamed these kitchen wagons as 'goulash cannons'. Many of these mobile kitchens were often towed by draught animals.

Infantry march forward towards the front. A typical infantry division consisted of three infantry regiments, an artillery regiment, reconnaissance, anti-tank, pioneer, and signal battalions, plus divisional services. Trucks transported much of the supporting battalions, but there were many infantry that marched on foot, including all the supply columns that were horse-drawn.

An Sd.Kfz.7 in mud during the spring thaw. The Sd.Kfz.7 prime mover used as a personnel carrier for towing mainly heavy ordnance comprised of three seats forward, three alongside the driver, and seating bunks in two more rows aft of four seats each for twelve soldiers including the driver. The equipment, ammunition, various provisions and supplies were stored in the rear compartment, which had a useable deck above for storage.

Two photos showing vehicles including an Sd.Kfz.7 halftrack struggling along a muddy road during the spring thaw in 1942. The road system in central Russia had caused immense logistical problems for the Panzerwaffe.

A Pz.Kpfw.III can be seen next to a pontoon bridge. Because of the large numbers of rivers and streams encountered during operations on the German central front all kinds of bridging and river crossings were essential if the Germans were to successfully achieve their objectives.

An SdKfz.7 advances along a road towing a 10cm schwere Kanone 18 to the front. Before the war the Wehrmacht had wanted a new 10.5cm gun as well as 15cm howitzer which were to share the same carriage. This also led to the 15cm sFH 18 being manufactured. Since both ordnances had a similar weight, they could be carried by a similar carriage minimising cost and giving the carriage dual action.

German infantry survey a decimated Russian tank following a tank battle with a Soviet unit. One of the crew members can be seen laying on the road evidently burnt to death.

A crew inside Sd.Kfz.7 hauling their 15cm howitzer to the front. The standard artillery organization consisted of some eight 15cm FH 18 howitzers. Each Abteilung comprised of three firing batteries with each battery containing four howitzers.

A 15cm field howitzer being towed by a prime mover across a pontoon bridge. Although the 15cm howitzer proved a success against enemy targets, by mid-1942, crews found the weapon too heavy. By 1943, only a few of these guns remained in active service and were used mainly in Russia until the end of the war.

A column of Pz.Kpfw.IV can be see advancing through a town in late 1942. During this period of the war the Pz.Kpfw.IV played a prominent role in the desperate attempt to halt strong Soviet counterattacks. Even though these powerful tanks were to be eventually outnumbered they were an ultimate credit to the panzer divisions they served.

A whitewashed prime mover can be seen fording a river during defensive action in late 1942. Navigating the vast terrain in central Russia with the lack of proper road signs and good road surfaces slowed the Panzerwaffe from achieving success in a number of places. In many areas, crews were hindered by the lack of maps. A number of units were compelled to move using nothing more than their compass and reports from aerial reconnaissance.

An Sd.Kfz.251 and Sd.Kfz.250 operating in central Russia in 1942, more than likely during a reconnaissance mission. The Sd.Kfz.250 was designed purely to provide armoured reconnaissance troops in the Panzer and Panzergrenadier divisions with good off-road performance. These light armoured personnel carriers normally carried six troops and were armed with either an MG 34 or MG 42 machine gun, complete with splinter shield.

An Sd.Kfz.251 Ausf.A with crew. The Sd.Kfz.251 had become not just a halftrack intended to simply transport infantry to the edge of the battlefield, but also a fully-fledged fighting vehicle.

A unit of Sd.Kfz.251 halftracks carrying Panzergrenadiers into battle enter a town. During the last two years of the war, the number of Panzergrenadier divisions grew and they soon earned the respect of being called the Panzer Elite. With the mounting losses of men and armour, the Panzergrenadiers displayed outstanding ability and endurance in the face of overwhelming odds.

An Sd.Kfz.251/8 Ausf.C Krankenpanzerwagen armoured ambulance passes a stationary Volkswagen Kübelwagen through a town that has seen extensive fighting. This halftrack was capable of carrying up to eight seated casualties or four seated casualties and two stretcher cases.

German personnel during a brief halt in operations can be seen standing next to an Sd.Kfz.251/1 Ausf.B. This was the standard personnel carrier and around 350 of these were produced up to mid-1940. Not many of these halftracks operated on the Eastern Front by 1942.

An Sd.Kfz.252 and StuG.III can be seen on a road. The Leichter Gepanzerter Munitionstransportwagen Sd.Kfz.252 was a light armoured ammunition carrier. A total of 413 vehicles were manufactured and issued as ammunition resupply vehicles to Sturmartillerie batteries and saw extensive operation in Russia. Note the national flag draped over the bonnet of the halftrack for aerial recognition.

A photograph showing the new Panzerjäger 38t fur 7.62cm PaK.36r Marder III. While the Pz.Kpfw.38(t) had largely become obsolete by early 1942, there were still many vehicles readily available for conversion into tank killers of Panzerjäger. The Germans had also stockpiled many captured Soviet 76.2mm field guns in large quantities, and a decision was made to bolt this gun to the Pz.Kpfw.38(t). As a result, mass production of what was called the Marder.III commenced, and a modified superstructure was bolted onto the standard tank chassis. These vehicles operated in special self-propelled anti-tank battalions (Panzerjäger-Abteilungen Sfl.) and were formed and equipped with the new Marder III. Both the Wehrmacht and the Waffen-SS fielded these battalions.

A column of Pz.Kpfw.IV Ausf.Gs advance along a road. The introduction of the Pz.Kpw.IV Ausf.G variant was intended to change the Pz.Kpfw.IVs overall combat role. While all previous versions were primarily intended as support tanks, attacking fortified positions in support of the panzer divisions, the Ausf.G was to receive a huge increase in firepower against armoured targets.

Chapter Four

First Rzhev–Sychyovka Offensive

Despite German resilience in front of Moscow in November and December 1941, the winter battles had left their infantry and panzer divisions battered, but they remained in reasonable shape. Although conditions had deteriorated along the front during the winter, it did allow several panzer units enough strength with sufficient supplies to launch a number of counterattacks. However, due to heavy Soviet counterattacks around Moscow it had driven German divisions back towards the city Rzhev, 140-miles west of Moscow. As a result, Rzhev became an important strategic defensive position for the Germans. By the spring of 1942, the city stood in a salient that protruded from the front lines, pointing towards Moscow. The Red Army were determined to safeguard the capital from another German attack and in order to achieve this, they wanted to push them away from Moscow.

The Germans were totally aware that Rzhev was a strategic crossroads and a vital rail junction which ran along the Volga River. It was the only town of major importance for many miles and the German 9th Army were determined to hold on to it. The 9th Army saw major fighting during Operation Typhoon, and saw action on the northern flank as the German 2nd, 3rd and 4th Panzer Armies and the 4th Army spearheaded the offensive on Moscow. However, by the spring of 1942, it was now on the defensive. The 9th Army commanded by Field Marshal Model, comprised of numerous dedicated tank destroyer battalions, known as Panzerjäger-Abteilung. The battalions, because of the erosion of German panzer units in certain armies, meant that the tank destroyers were usually attached individually to divisions. In the 9th Army, where tank losses had been high, there was a high concentration of tank destroyer battalions which included the 5th Tank Destroyer Battalion, 8th Tank Destroyer Battalion, 28th Anti-Tank Battalion, 102nd Tank Destroyer Battalion, 106th Tank Destroyer Battalion, 129th Tank Destroyer Battalion, 206th Tank Destroyer Battalion, 236th Tank Destroyer Battalion, 241st Tank Destroyer Battalion, 251st Tank Destroyer Battalion, and the 256th Tank Destroyer Battalion.

The 9th Army spent the duration between April and July 1942 fighting a series of defensive actions along its front in the Rzhev Salient. Its primary objective was to stem and cut off Russian supply lines and to reduce their ability to destroy Army Group Centre. During this period, German formations managed to recover sufficiently and mount several operations to clear their rear area. In fact, they were so successful, that in July they made plans to mount a large-scale offensive to destroy what was left of the Soviet armies dug in along their front opposite the Rzhev Salient. If they succeeded, the Germans would once again be able to drive their formations towards Moscow and put the city under immediate threat. The Russians were totally aware that the central sector of the Eastern Front posed the greatest threat. German forces at Rzhev represented a growing danger that Moscow could once again be threatened. In view of this imminent threat, Zhukov convinced Stalin to give him additional forces in the area in front of the Russian capital. After agreeing in August, Stalin asked General Zhukov and General Konev, commanding the West Front and the Kalinin Front respectively, to carry out a strategic offensive to retake Rzhev and to strike Army Group Centre, driving them back so its forces would no longer pose an immediate threat to Moscow. The offensive was to fall upon one of the Soviet's primary opponents, the 9th Army.

At the end of July, the 9th Army had sixteen infantry divisions organised in three corps: fourteen of these divisions were in the line, one in reserve and another in transit. The army comprised of General Carl Hilpert's XXIII Corps with the 197th Division, 246th Division, 86th Division, 110th Division, 129th Division and 253rd Division, General Bruno Bieler's VI Corps with the 206th Division, 251st Division, 87th Division and 256th Division; and General and General Hans Zorn's XLVI Panzerkorps with the 14th Division (mot.), 161st Division, 36th Division (mot.) and 342nd Division. The army's reserves were the 6th Division and part of the 328th Division.

Confronting the 9th Army was the Red Army's Kalinin Front which comprised of eleven infantry divisions, three infantry brigades, eight tank brigades and ten artillery regiments. Reserve formations were also incorporated into the order of battle which contained five infantry divisions, six tank brigades, two artillery regiments, four anti-tank artillery regiments, and ten battalions of 'Katyusha' rocket launchers. The majority of the Soviet tank strength comprised of various separate tank brigades, which were organised for the direct support of the infantry. To launch the offensive, the 30th Army used nine tank brigades operating 390 tanks, the 31st Army had six tank brigades with 274 tanks, and the 20th Army had five tank brigades with 255 tanks.

The Red Army's objective was to destroy the Rzhev Salient. Army Group Centre had already heavily fortified the salient with a mass of mine belts, trenches, bunkers, anti-tank guns, and machine gun emplacements. The well-constructed road network also allowed the rapid movement of reinforcements to the area.

The Soviet offensive was launched on 30 July during the early hours of the morning with a massive artillery attack. The artillery attack's aim was to soften the German positions in order to allow company and battalion sized infantry raids into the German defensive positions all along the front. Almost immediately, across vast parts of Army Group Centre, the front line erupted in a wall of flame and smoke. Hundreds of guns, mortars, and Katyusha multiple rocket launchers poured fire and destruction onto the Rzhev Salient. Shell after shell thundered into the German strong points. In some sectors of the front, German soldiers, fearing complete destruction, scrambled out of their trenches to save themselves from the rain of bombs. Yet, in spite of the heavy bombardment, most of the German front was solid and fought back with ferocity. Massive Red Army losses were sustained by units trying to storm the German defences. However, the Russians were determined to try and crush the salient. Over the course of a number of days there were continued Soviet tank attacks which were employing new tactics of remaining out of the range of the German anti-tank guns and shelling every German position.

In order to apply more pressure on the German defences, Zhukov planned to break through the German line at Pogoreloye Gorodishche, advance toward the Vazuza River, and destroy the defending forces of Zorn's XLVI Panzer Corps.

On 4 August, Zhukov launched his West Front's attack against the Rzhev Salient and sent T-34s towards the Pogoreloye Gorodishche strongpoint which was being ardently held by the 364th Infantry Regiment of the 161st Division. Supporting the regiment was a hodgepodge of armour comprising of Pz.Kpf.IIIs and IVs. The Soviet attack stormed the position and soon overwhelmed the German defences, capturing Pogoreloye Gorodishche.

As the situation spiralled out of control for the Germans, Hitler immediately authorised the release of five divisions comprising of lots of armour. These included the 1st Panzer Division, 2nd Panzer Division, 5th Panzer Division, and the 102nd Division and 78th Division. When these panzer divisions arrived, they were immediately put into action. The 5th Panzer Division for instance was rushed to the crucial sector in the area to the north of Sychevka, where its forward elements crossed the Vazuza River at Chlepen and then fanned out, and hurriedly occupied defensive positions. Simultaneously, the 2nd Panzer Division undertook wide, sweeping, deep penetrating attacks using Pz.Kpfw.IVs to drive back enemy infantry. The 1st Panzer Division, which had received a new batch of Pz.Kpfw.IVs tanks, also heavily attacked advancing enemy forces, which included numerous T-34 tanks supported by thousands of infantrymen.

By 17 August the 9th Army's losses had reached almost 20,000 men and by the end of the month, they were on the point of collapse. The panzer divisions had each lost between 1,500 and 2,000 men, along with the majority of the tanks. The 3rd Panzer Army reported losses of more than 10,000 men.

Red Army losses were catastrophic, and due to the resilience of the Germans defending the salient, the Red Army called off the offensive and went over to the defensive. By 10 September, the Soviet armies had almost been completely decimated in the area. They had been reduced to half-strength, with 184,265 men and 306 tanks. Yet, in spite of the huge losses on both sides, fighting continued until the beginning of October 1942. The battle for the Rzhev Salient had been a contest of attrition for both sides, with massive casualties for little gain. Although the Germans were still holding on to the salient, they would no longer be strong enough to resume an offensive against Moscow. Over the course of five months, Army Group Centre would be stagnated along the front, replenishing its forces.

Three photographs depicting General Field Marshal Walter Model, who had commanded the 3rd Panzer Division at the start of 'Barbarossa', and had become commander of the XLI Corps (mot.) in October 1941. He had shown great resolve in the winter's defensive battles, and was promoted to command the 9th Army on 12 January 1942. Model was a tough soldier and a specialist in defensive warfare. Model had been a very successful Eastern Front commander and his ability to adapt to constantly changing conditions on the battlefield earned him much respect among his men. He was a master of defence whom Hitler would later come to rely as his 'trouble shooter' and 'fire fighter'. His ingenuity enabled him to salvage apparently hopeless situations and perform amazing tasks by holding the line at all costs. Although he had a paradoxical personality, he had absolute trust of the German leader and those that fought for him. Out on the battlefield in front of his men, Model was energetic, courageous and innovative, and friendly with his enlisted men.

A Pz.Kpfw.III has halted in a field whilst German troops round up Russian PoWs following heavy fighting in the Rzhev Salient in July 1942. On 2 July 1942, the 9th Army launched Operation Seydlitz with a sole objective of clearing out Russian forces in the area. The Germans first blocked the natural breakout route through the Obsha valley and proceeded to wrench open Russian forces into two isolated pockets. The operation by the Germans was a complete success and saw thousands of Russian troops isolated, captured, and killed.

A Marder.II advancing across a field. This tank destroyer was part of the 9th Army which comprised of a high concentration of tank destroyer battalions.

The crew of a Marder II pose for the camera next to their tank destroyer. On 1 April 1942, it was designated as the 7.62cm PaK 36(r) auf Fgst. PzKpfw.II(F) (Sfl.). However, two months later it was renamed as the Pz.Sfl.1 fuer 7.62cm PaK 36 (Sd.Kfz.132). Further designations followed, but the machine remained generally unchanged. The second version of the Marder.II was known as the Panzerkampwagen II als Sfl. Mit 7.5cm PaK 40 'Marder II' (Sd.Kfz.131). The tank hunter was based on a modified Pz.Kpfw.II Ausf.F tank chassis. Its design comprised of converting the tank and mounting a PaK 40 on the tank chassis. Production of these vehicles began at the same time as the first version of the Marder.II. They were quickly sent to the Eastern Front.

A well supplied Pz.Kpfw.III can be seen advancing along a dusty road bound for the front.

(**Above**) A Pz.Kpfw.III Ausf.H on the central front in the summer of 1942. This Ausf.H tank looked almost identical to the Ausf.G variant. The biggest change made to the Ausf.H was the addition of extra 30mm armour plates on the hull front and rear and on the superstructure front. This gave the tank 60mm armour that was effectively immune to fire from the main anti-tank guns in use in 1941 and early 1942, but did increase the weight of the tank. To compensate for the extra weight, the Ausf.H used the 40cm wide tracks first used late in the production of the Ausf.G. These wider tracks also required a redesign of the wheels. Stronger torsion bars were added at the same time, as was a new transmission.

(**Opposite**) Two photographs taken showing the Pz.Kpfw.III Ausf.J during operations on the central front in the summer of 1942. This Ausf.J was the ninth variant of the Pz.Kpfw.III medium tank family. The Ausf.J looked very similar to the Ausf.G and H. It was designed with a turret housing a 5cm KwK 38 L/42 tank gun. The hull frontal armour thickness had been increased to 50mm. An additional armour plate was installed internally to the front of the turret in the spring of 1941, increasing it to a maximum thickness of 57mm in certain parts of the chassis. To improve engine compartment ventilation, the structure of the chassis was extended. The armoured front brake vents were redesigned. On the roof of the turret was an armoured extractor fan. The 50cm KwK 38 L/42 tank gun was capable of firing up to twenty rounds per minute, through the use of a semi-automatic breech that opened before the end of the recoil, ejected the used casing, and allowed for fast loading of the next shell.

An MG 34 crew along a defensive position on the Rzhev Salient in the summer of 1942. A Soviet tank has been knocked out of action. The area of Rzhev comprised of open farmed land with a number of small villages, which often contained numerous houses along the roadside. The roads were mostly mud tracks that became almost impassable when it rained, but normally dried out in the summer time, but were still in terrible condition. This often led tank crews, both German and Russian, to advance across open fields but they became sitting targets to anti-tank gunners.

An early variant StuG.III Ausf.B rolling along a road during the summer of 1942. By the end of September 1942, Army Group Centre consisted of twenty-five divisions – half the army group strength – including twenty infantry and four panzer, as well as the famous Grossdeutchland Division.

Sd.Kfz.7/1 halftrack mounting a quadruple 2cm flak gun Flugzeugabwehrkanone 30. These flak guns gave an even greater effectiveness at combating the ever-increasing speeds of low-altitude enemy fighting bombers and attack aircraft. Each of the four guns had a separate magazine that held only twenty rounds. This meant that a maximum combined rate of fire of 1,400 rounds per minute was reduced practically to 800 rounds per minute for combat use. This would still require an emptied magazine's replacement every six seconds, on each of the four guns.

An Sd.Kfz.11 can be seen towing a 10.5cm field artillery gun towards the front. The main role of this prime mover was to tow medium ordnance such as the 3.7cm FlaK 43 anti-aircraft gun and the 10.5cm leFH 18 field howitzer. It could carry eight troops in addition to towing a gun or trailer.

An Sd.Kfz.251 halftrack motors along a road. The crew have applied foliage to the vehicle in order to help conceal it from both ground and aerial observation. By the late summer of 1942, German armoured crews discovered that camouflage was the key to survival against the growing might of their enemy.

Chapter Five

Aftermath

By March 1943, Army Group Centre decided to implement a series of local retreats from the Rzhev Salient. This retreat was in anticipation of another possible Soviet offensive. The shortening of the German front from the salient reduced the line by 230 miles and released twenty-one divisions. The withdrawal from the salient allowed Soviet troops to enter the city of Rzhev without meeting any resistance. What followed was a series of Red Army advances in the area which saw them occupy numerous towns and villages in the salient, including taking control of Olenino, Gzhatsk, Sychyovka, Bely, and Vyazma. In some areas of the front, the Germans had not withdrawn completely and fought a number of battles.

The shortening of the German lines in the salient was a tactical move and successfully allowed German infantry and armour to create a reserve for operations along other parts of the front.

With the withdrawal of Army Group Centre, the Red Army once again wanted to take full advantage of the situation and made a number of co-ordinated assaults to the south of Rzhev in the Kursk region. The Russians wanted to try to outflank the Germans as they shortened their front lines. However, yet again, they overestimated the strength and resilience of the German forces in Army Group Centre. Eventually, the Soviet attacks from Kursk towards Orel failed to make progress. As a result, the offensive was called off and front lines once again stagnated.

Throughout the first half of 1943, Army Group Centre had maintained more or less the strategic initiative on the Eastern Front. However, by this point, it had completely lost any chance of resuming any type of offensive against Moscow. After its forces had shortened its line from the Rzhev Salient, its strategy had changed. Its forces were now becoming stronger and reserves were replenishing the losses from the previous winter. There appeared once again optimism on the Eastern Front. For this reason, Hitler was confronted with a tempting strategic opportunity that he was convinced would yield him victory. This victory, he thought, would be achieved at Kursk. It would prove to be the last great German offensive on the Eastern Front. The attack would be launched against a huge salient at Kursk measuring some 120 miles wide and 75 miles deep.

However, by July 1943, when the Germans launched their long-awaited summer offensive codenamed 'Operation Zitadelle', the war in the East changed forever. Within two weeks of the attack, the Red Army had repulsed the German forces with considerable losses. In August, just weeks after the German failure at Kursk, the Red Army counterattacked towards Orel and Kharkov and launched a massive attack against Army Group Centre. For nearly three months, the Russians fought a series of heavy clashes against the Centre and managed to recapture Smolensk and the rail junction at Nevel, forcing back the Germans on a broad front. However, the Russian attack soon faltered in the Vitebsk-Orsha-Mogilev area where almost impregnable lines of defence had been erected by the Germans.

In November 1943, further Red Army assaults were made against Army Group Centre in the Gomel and Orsha area. The fighting raged for months, but the Russians were again unsuccessful against the strong 'Ostwall' defences. During the first months of 1944, Army Group Centre continued to endure repeated heavy attacks, but found the mass of well dug-in defences almost too difficult to break. By the spring of 1944, the Soviet command began to draw up plans for a massive concentration of forces along the entire frontline in central Russia. The new summer offensive was to be called 'Operation Bagration' and its attack would annihilate Army Group Centre once and for all.

Whitewashed Pz.Kpfw.IIIs out in the snow during operations on the central front in early 1943. Within months this panzer was slowly relegated from the front lines to secondary minor combat roles, such as training. It was finally replaced as the main German medium tank by the Pz.Kpfw.IV and the new Pz.Kpfw.V Panther that made its debut at Kursk in July 1943.

A white washed Pz.Kpfw.IV in late 1942 or early 1943. The Pz.Kpfw.IV continued to play an important role during operations in 1943, including supporting units that were withdrawing to new defence lines. This tank remained the core of Germany's armoured divisions, including operating in numerous Waffen-SS Panzer divisions.

A crewman with his whitewashed Pz.Kpfw.IV during operations in Army Group Centre in the early winter of 1943. In March 1943, the 9th Army evacuated the Rzhev Salient as part of a general shortening of the line. The objective of this withdrawal was to create a reserve for operations elsewhere along the front. These formations were later used during the 1943 summer campaign, resulting in the Battle of Kursk. Although the shortening of the line was a success, there would be no possibility of going back over to the offensive and resuming operations against Moscow. Capturing the Soviet capital had now been lost forever.

A motorcyclist is struggling with his machine during winter operations. Not only was travelling on the ice, snow, and mud hazardous, but during 1942 there had been an increased casualty rate among motorcyclists. As a consequence, a number of Kradschützen battalions were disbanded and transferred into the panzer reconnaissance battalions or Aufklärungsabteilung. During 1942 and early 1943 these reconnaissance battalions had become highly mobile motorized infantry with panzer divisions being equipped with motorcycle combinations such as the BMW R75, Zundapp KS 750, supported by the Volkswagen Kubelwagens and Sd.Kfz.221/222/223 light armoured cars. As with all German combat formations, the composition of the Aufklärungsabteilung varied from division to division.

The first of three photographs showing the Marder.III Ausf.M both during winter and early summer operations in 1943. This vehicle was the variant based on the Geschützwagen 38(t) Ausf.M, a purpose-designed vehicle for self-propelled gun use. It was again armed with the 7.5cm PaK 40 anti-tank gun. The Ausf.M was the final variant of the Marder series, and was a significant improvement over previous models, with its lower silhouette, sloped armour, and much more functional fighting compartment. Crews soon reported its tactical worth, as it was more than capable of destroying Soviet T-34 tanks. These tank hunters extensively served with the divisional anti-tank battalions and proved very successful at countering Russian armour.

The crew of a Pz.Kpfw.IV Ausf.G pose for the camera during operations on the central Front in early Spring 1943. The Ausf.G variant was introduced in 1942 and received a huge increase in firepower against armoured targets. Apart from its main rearmament, very little had changed in its overall design compared to the previous version. The introduction of these panzers helped the overstretched German armoured divisions more effectively fight against powerful Soviet tanks that were being fielded in their thousands on the Eastern Front.

A photograph showing personnel inside the interior compartment of the Sd.Kfz.251. This halftrack was designed mainly to carry troops and equipment, with a focus on functionality and practicality. The troop compartment typically included benches for soldiers, storage lockers, and mounting points for weapons like the MG 34 or MG 42 machine gun.

The crew pose for the camera with a new Sd.Kfz.251/9 – Schützenpanzerwagen (7.5cm KwK 37 L/24) 'Stummel'. This halftrack mounted a short-barrel 7.5cm howitzer, which used the same mounting as the StuG.III. It was nicknamed 'Stummel' or 'Stump', and was committed in great numbers on the Eastern Front.

An Sd.Kfz.11 prime mover can be seen operating during an operation in the spring of 1943. The halftrack, for carrying personnel and supplies, was entered from the rear of the vehicle.

A Pz.Kpfw.III complete with Schürzen side plates can be seen rolling along a road. These side plates were mounted on rails along the sides of the tanks, creating a spaced armour effect. This spaced armour helped to deflect or break up projectiles like those from Soviet 14.5mm anti-tank rifles, preventing them from penetrating the main hull armour. While not designed to defeat shaped charge projectiles like HEAT rounds, they were effective against kinetic energy rounds.

An interesting photograph showing a well concealed Pz.Kpfw.IV Ausf.G complete with intact Schurzen. The crew have camouflaged the tank with foliage. Although difficult to see, it appears another Pz.Kpfw.IV has been concealed in the same way behind it.

An interesting photograph showing a Pz.Kpfw.III Ausf.N on the battlefield supported by Sd.Kfz.251 halftracks. The Ausf.N was the final production version of the standard Pz.Kpfw.III, and the only version to be armed with the 7.5cm KwK L/24 gun. This gun had been used on early versions of the Pz.Kpfw.IV from Ausf.A to Ausf.F1, and fired a more effective high explosive round than the long barrelled 5cm gun, as well as being able to fire a shaped-charge round. From March 1943, the Ausf.N was fitted with 5mm thick side skirts or Schürzen.

Panzergrenadiers pose for the camera next to an Sd.Kfz.251 halftrack. The Sd.Kfz.251 was a medium armoured halftrack with 6 to 12mm of sloped armoured plates. It had one or two MG 34 or MG 42 machine guns to support an assault or for local defence. It was open-topped and had only one door at the back of the vehicle for quick access or exit.

A panzer crew can be seen standing next to an Sd.Kfz.251 Ausf.D halftrack. The Sd.Kfz.251 came in four variants, from A to D, and every version had its own upgrade. The halftrack had a crew of two, which comprised of a driver and radio operator/navigator, who can be seen inside the halftrack. The vehicle carried a single squad of ten panzergrenadiers. Panzer divisions relied heavily on Wehrmacht infantry support so these halftracks were ideal to transport soldiers to the front where they could be utilised on the battlefield at speed.

German Order of Battle June 1941

Army Group Centre (General von Bock)

9th Army (General Strauss)

XXXXII Army-Corps (CO: General Kuntze)

87th Infantry-Division	1st SS-Mot Infantry
102nd Infantry-Division	106th Infantry-Division
129th Infantry-Division	110th Infantry-Division

Panzergruppe.III (General Hoth)

XXXIX Army-Corps (mot.) (General Schmidt)

69th Artillery-Regiment (mot.)	Luftwaffe Flak-Unit. 84
Luftwaffe Flak-Unit. I./36	20th Panzer-Division
605th FlaK-Battalion	Luftwaffe Flak-Unit. 74
643rd Panzerjäger-Unit	14th Motorized-Infantry-Division
7th Panzer-Division	20th Motorized-Infantry-Division

LVII Army-Corps (mot.) (General Kuntzen)

Luftwaffe-Flak-Unit. I./29	19th Panzer-Division
12th Panzer-Division	Luftwaffe Flak-Unit. 85
Luftwaffe Flak-Unit. 75	18th Motorized-Infantry-Division

4th Army (General von Kluge)

VII Army-Corps (General Fahrenbacher)

41st Artillerie-Regt. (mot.)	23rd Infantry-Division
203rd StuG-Unit	258th Infantry-Division
529th Panzerjäger-Unit	268th Infantry-Division
7th Infantry-Division	221st Security-Division

IX Army-Corps (General Geyer)

622nd Artillery-Regiment (mot.)	263rd Infantry-Division
226th StuG-Unit	292nd Infantry-Division
137th Infantry-Division	

XIII Army-Corps (General Felber)

17th Infantry-Division	78th Infantry-Division

XXXXIII Army-Corps (General Heinrici)

697th Artillery-Regiment (mot.)	131st Infantry-Division
786th Artillery-Regiment (mot.)	134th Infantry-Division
611th FlaK-Battalion	252nd Infantry-Division

Panzergruppe.II (General Guderian)

Luftwaffe-FlaK-Corps I (General von Axthelm)

Luftwaffe Flak-Regiment 101
Luftwaffe Flak-Regiment 104
Luftwaffe Flak-Battalion 77

Luftwaffe Flak-Battalion 77
Luftwaffe Flak-Battalions I./12, I./22, I./11, II./11

XII Army-Corps (General Schroth)

617th Artillery-Regiment (mot.)
788th Artillery-Regiment (mot.)
279th Flak-Artillery-Battalion
610th FlaK-Battalion
192nd StuG-Unit
201st StuG-Unit

654th Panzerjäger-Battalion (mot.)
Pioneer-Regiment (mot.) 507
31st Infantry-Division
34th Infantry-Division
45th Infantry-Division

XXIV Army-Corps (mot.) (General von Schweppenburg)

623rd Artillery-Regiment (mot.)
'Lehr' (mot.)
521st Panzer-Jäger. (Sfl.)
Pioneer-Regiment (mot.) 515
3rd Panzer-Division

4th Panzer-Division
10th Motorized-Infantry-Division
1st Cavalry-Division
267th Infantry-Division

XXXXVI Army-Corps (mot.) (General von Vietinghoff)

Pioneer-Regiment 513
10th Panzer-Division
2nd SS-Mot Infantry-Division 'Reich'

XXXXVII Army Corps (mot.) (General Lemelsen)

792 Artillery-Regiment. (mot.)
611th Panzer-Jäger-Battalion
100th Flammpanzer-Battalion.
Pioneer-Regiment (mot.) 413

17th Panzer-Division
18th Panzer-Division
29th Motorized-Infantry-Division
167th Infantry-Division

Russian Order of Battle 22 June 1941

Soviet Front
(Main Russian Forces)

Western Front (Colonel General D.G. Pavlov)

3 Army (Headquarters only)

2 Rifle Corps (Major General A.N. Ermakov)
100 Rifle Division	161 Rifle Division

21 Rifle Corps (Major General V.B. Borisov)
17 Rifle Division	37 Rifle Division
24 Rifle Division	

44 Rifle Corps (Major General V.A. Yushkevich)
64 Rifle Division	108 Rifle Division

47 Rifle Corps (Major General S.I. Povetkin)
50 Rifle Division	121 Rifle Division
55 Rifle Division	143 Rifle Division

4 Airborne Corps (Major General A.S. Zhandov)
7 Airborne Brigade	214 Airborne Brigade
8 Airborne Brigade	8 Antitank Brigade

17 Mechanized Corps (36 tanks) (Major General M.P. Petrov)
27 Tank Division	209 Motorized Division
36 Tank Division	2 Motorcycle Regiment

20 Mechanized Corps (93 tanks) (Major General A.G. Niktin)
26 Tank Division	210 Motorized Division
38 Tank Division	24 Motorcycle Regiment

3 Army (Lieutenant General V.I.Kuznetsov)
4 Rifle Corps	56 Rifle Division
27 Rifle Division	85 Rifle Division

11 Mechanized Corps (Major General D.K. Mostevenko)
29 Tank Division	16 Motorcycle Regiment
33 Tank Division	7 Antitank Brigade
204 Motorized Division	

4 Army (Lieutenant General A.A. Korobkov)

28 Rifle Corps (Major General V.S. Popov)

6 Rifle Division	49 Rifle Division
42 Rifle Division	75 Rifle Division

14 Mechanized Corps (Major General S.I. Oborin) 22 Tank Division

30 Tank Division	20 Motorcycle Regiment
205 Motorized Division	

10 Army (Major General K.D. Golubev)

1 Rifle Corps (Major General F.D. Rubsev)

2 Rifle Division	8 Rifle Division

5 Rifle Corps (Major General A,V, Gamov)

13 Rifle Division	113 Rifle Division
85 Rifle Division	

6 Cavalry Corps (Major General I.S. Nikitin)

6 Cavalry Division	155 Rifle Division
36 Cavalry Division	

6 Mechanized Corps (Major General M.G. Khatskilevich)

4 Tank Division	29 Mechanized Division
7 Tank Division	4 Motorcycle Regiment

13 Mechanized Corps (Major General P.N. Akhliustin)

25 Tank Division	208 Mechanized Division
31 Tank Division	18 Motorcycle Regiment